SCIENCE MISSIONS

Developing Flu Vaccines

Michael Burgan

www.raintreepublishers.co.uk
Visit our website to find out more information about Raintree books.

To order:
☎ Phone 0845 6044371
📄 Fax +44 (0) 1865 312263
📧 Email myorders@raintreepublishers.co.uk

Customers from outside the UK please telephone +44 1865 312262

Raintree is an imprint of Capstone Global Library Limited, a company incorporated in England and Wales having its registered office at 7 Pilgrim Street, London, EC4V 6LB – Registered company number: 6695582

Edited by Adam Miller, Andrew Farrow, and Adrian Vigliano
Designed by Philippa Jenkins
Original illustrations © Capstone Global Library Ltd (2011)
Illustrated by KJA-artists.com
Picture research by Tracy Cummins
Production control by Alison Parsons
Originated by Dot Gradations
Printed and bound in China by South China Printing Company Ltd

ISBN 978 1 406217 57 5 (hardback)
14 13 12 11 10
10 9 8 7 6 5 4 3 2 1

ISBN 978 1 406220 25 4 (paperback)
15 14 13 12 11
10 9 8 7 6 5 4 3 2 1

British Library Cataloguing in Publication Data
Burgan, Michael
Developing flu vaccines. – (Science missions)
615.3'72·dc22
A full catalogue record for this book is available from the British Library.

Acknowledgements
We would like to thank the following for permission to reproduce photographs: AP Images/Imaginechina/Chen xichun p.**37**; Alamy ©Robert Harding Picture Library Ltd p.**28**; AP Photo/Charles Dharapak pp.**46–47**; Corbis pp.**4–5**; Corbis ©DANIEL AGUILAR/Reuters p.**8**; Corbis ©Bettmann p.**9**; Corbis ©Hulton-Deutsch Collection p.**12**; Corbis ©CARLOS BARRIA p.**39**; Corbis ©CHARLES PLATIAU/Reuters p.**43**; Corbis/Reuters/James Gathany/CDC p.**44**; Getty Images p.**7**; Getty Images/Leon Neall/AFP pp.**10–11**; Getty Images/AFP/NORBERT MILLAUER pp.**18–19**; Getty Images/Popperfoto p.**21**; Getty Images/Dr. Gopal Murti pp.**24–25**; Getty Images/AFP/MARIO VAZQUEZ p.**30**; Getty Images/Mario Villafuerte p.**34**; Getty Images/Kallista Images p.**45**; istockphoto ©Stephen Sweet p.**48**; Photo Researchers, Inc./National Physical Laboratory/Crown Copyright p.**16**; Photo Researchers, Inc. p.**20**; Photo Researchers, Inc./James King-Holmes pp.**32–33**; Photo Researchers, Inc./Ray Simons pp.**40–41**; Photolibrary/Custom Medical Stock p.**14**; Shutterstock ©Erwin Wodicka p.**15**; Shutterstock ©Bork p.**22**; Shutterstock ©Sebastian Kaulitzki pp.**50–51**; University of Maryland Communications p.**31**.

Cover photograph of bird flu research in China reproduced with permission of AP Photo/Xinhua, Cui Feng.

We would like to thank Marc Solomon for his invaluable help in the preparation of this book.

Disclaimer

CONTENTS

Some words are printed in bold, **like this**. You can find out what they mean by looking in the glossary. You can also look out for them in the **WORD STORE** box at the bottom of each page.

DEADLY VIRUS

"I see hundreds of young men in the uniform of their country coming into the hospital in groups of 10 or more. They are placed on cots until every bed is full and yet others crowd in. The faces soon wear a bluish cast; a distressing cough brings up blood-stained fluid. In the morning the dead bodies are stacked about like cord wood.**"**

US doctor Victor Vaughan worked for the US Army and described the effects of the 1918 pandemic.

In 1918 US soldiers trained to fight in World War I (1914–18). But tens of thousands of them never saw the war. A powerful disease spread through their camps, forcing many into bed. The illness caused soaring temperatures and aching bodies.

The disease seemed similar to influenza, also called the flu, a sickness known for hundreds of years. But this new illness was a far deadlier form of the flu. In some cases, patients developed a lung disease called **pneumonia**. With their bodies already weak, they could not fight off the flu once it reached their lungs. Their lungs filled with fluid, making it hard to breathe. As patients neared death, blood sometimes flowed from their noses.

First reports of the new flu came from Spain and several other countries. The disease seemed to be an **epidemic**, which is the quick spread of a disease in one area. It soon became a **pandemic**, meaning it spread around the world.

From Europe, soldiers of many nations and non-military people carried the disease to every continent except Antarctica. By the time the pandemic ended, the flu had killed more soldiers than the war had.

No medical answers

The 1918 influenza created fear wherever it spread. Young people in good health seemed to die almost instantly. Some elderly people suffered heart attacks as they strained to get air into their diseased lungs. Doctors did not know how this new version of the flu was different from what they had seen before, and they had no way to fight it. They thought a micro-organism was causing the illness. A micro-organism is a very tiny living creature. But they had no tools to find it and began to look for a treatment.

Understanding influenza

The terrible flu pandemic finally ended in 1919. When it was over, more than 40 million people had died. Scientists would take almost 15 years to finally discover that a virus causes influenza.

In the decades that followed, researchers developed substances called vaccines to prevent the flu. They also created medicines that could help patients fight the disease if they caught it.

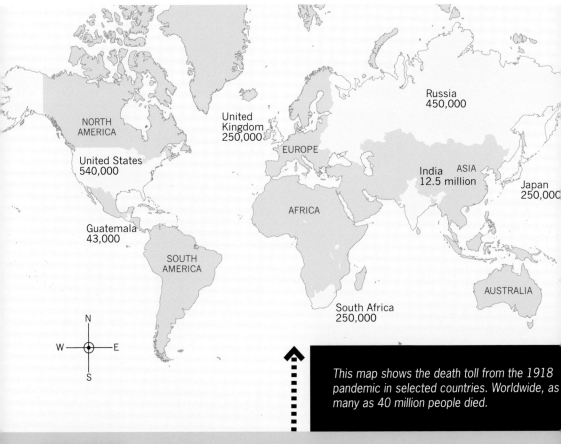

Russia
450,000

NORTH
AMERICA

United
Kingdom
250,000

EUROPE

United States
540,000

India
12.5 million

ASIA

Japan
250,000

AFRICA

Guatemala
43,000

SOUTH
AMERICA

South Africa
250,000

AUSTRALIA

N
W — E
S

This map shows the death toll from the 1918 pandemic in selected countries. Worldwide, as many as 40 million people died.

WORD STORE   **symptom** outward sign of a disease in an infected person

During the 1957 flu pandemic, improved research let governments prepare a vaccine in just six months.

Fears of new pandemics

Despite medical improvements, the world still faced dangerous flu pandemics. One appeared in 1957, and another in 1968. They were not as bad as the 1918 outbreak. But any pandemic creates problems. Schools and some businesses are often shut down, as officials try to stop the spread of the disease. In the worst cases, hospitals fill with people who cannot be treated at home. Scientists never know in advance if a pandemic virus will turn out to be a killer flu.

WHAT'S IN A NAME?

The word *influenza* is Italian for "influence". Hundreds of years ago, Europeans thought the position of the planets in the sky could influence human health and create flu **symptoms** (outward signs). Other people blamed diseases on evil spirits or other forces not explained by science. Modern science began to develop in the 1500s. Scientists found and explained the natural causes of diseases and began creating methods to treat them.

A medical challenge

Since 1918 doctors and researchers have worried about new deadly flu pandemics. The flu presents a unique medical problem. The illness is not caused by just one virus that always remains the same. The make-up of the influenza virus changes slightly over short periods of time. The flu you catch this year will probably not be the same one that made your friend ill the year before. "Super flu" viruses combine features of several different viruses, posing even more challenges.

A new pandemic emerges

Another deadly pandemic erupted in 2009. That March, reports began to come out of Mexico. Hundreds of people, many of them young, were catching the flu. Samples of the virus were sent to labs in Canada and the United States. The scientists soon learned the virus was a new kind of flu virus. It had genes similar to ones in flu viruses found in pigs. Because of this similarity, **media** such as newspapers and magazines soon called the new influenza the "swine flu."

Some Mexicans wore face masks when swine flu appeared in 2009. A report that year showed that wearing masks can offer some protection against influenza.

WORD STORE   **media** organizations that produce news reports

In 1976 US health officials feared a pandemic from a swine flu virus. A vaccine was quickly developed and the government planned to vaccinate the whole country. A few people, however, developed a disease called Guillain-Barré syndrome (GBS) after receiving their injections. Fears spread about the vaccine, and the government stopped the programme.

The pandemic never came, and scientists thought the GBS might have come from harmful **particles** that entered one batch of vaccine. In 2009 some media brought up the 1976 swine flu incident, which seemed to stir some fear of the new vaccine. Doctors, however, assured the public that the earlier GBS cases were a rare event and would probably not happen again.

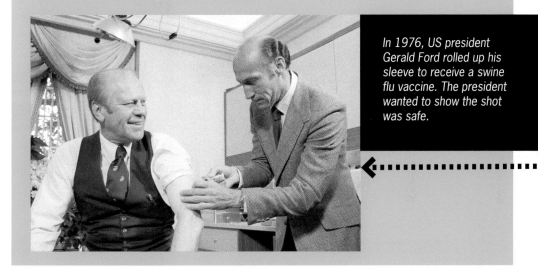

In 1976, US president Gerald Ford rolled up his sleeve to receive a swine flu vaccine. The president wanted to show the shot was safe.

As more cases were reported in more countries, scientists faced a tough task. They had to inform the world about the new flu, so people could try to prevent catching it. Yet they also did not want people to become overly afraid. The scientists needed time to learn how dangerous swine flu might be. Chris Olsen, a US scientist, said in April, "This is . . . not a good time to panic. Panic is not a useful response right now."

Still, worries increased in June 2009, as the flu struck in dozens of countries. It produced mild symptoms compared to the 1918 pandemic. But the swine flu still concerned health officials, as it marked the world's first flu pandemic in 41 years. Scientists around the world immediately began to develop vaccines to prevent the spread of swine flu.

WORD STORE   particle tiny piece of material

VIRUSES
AND
ILLNESSES

Before we see how scientists develop flu vaccines, let's take a look at what they are battling. Influenza is just one of many viruses. You might have already come in contact with some of the others that make people ill. A sore throat and a runny nose are among the first **symptoms** of a cold. That illness can be caused by one of several hundred viruses. Or if red spots start to pop up on your face, you could be ill with chicken pox, which is caused by a different virus.

Viruses are just one of several kinds of **pathogens**, or micro-organisms that cause disease. Other common pathogens are bacteria. These micro-organisms can cause skin rashes and ear infections, as well as other health problems. Viruses are all around us, including in the air, soil, and the sea, and they can infect plants and animals as well as humans. In their labs, scientists have discovered millions of different viruses. Many more are still unknown.

Viruses present a challenging puzzle to researchers. US government scientist Paul Mahoney says, "Viruses are strange **particles** that exist in the grey area between life and non-life." Viruses are the smallest known pathogens and can infect other micro-organisms, such as bacteria.

Halfway through 2009 the world prepared for a second wave of swine flu. Meanwhile, researchers raced to develop a testing kit that could be used to accurately diagnose the virus.

Viral invasion

A virus must invade the cells of a living creature, or organism, to reproduce (pass on) copies of itself. The invaded organism is called the host. Inside the host, the virus takes over a cell. Once the virus has control, it forces the cell to make more copies of the virus. These copies then invade other cells and continue to reproduce. The host's invaded cells cannot do what they are supposed to, such as control the function of the lungs or liver. The breakdown of the host's cells causes disease.

THE GERM THEORY

During the 1860s, French scientist Louis Pasteur (pictured below) helped prove what is called the germ theory of disease. He saw that some micro-organisms enter the body and harm it. Pasteur then proved that heat or chemicals could kill some bacteria that cause disease. He and other scientists of the time called the first known pathogens "germs," and the word is still often used today. The heating of liquids, such as milk, to kill germs is called pasteurization.

Pasteur's work influenced Joseph Lister, a British scientist. Lister began washing surgical tools and operating rooms with a chemical that killed bacteria. This process reduced the spread of disease in hospitals. Not all illnesses are caused by pathogens, but many are. The flu virus is just one of the "germs" that make people ill.

immune system parts of the body that fight disease
mucus slippery body fluid

COLD OR FLU?

Some people confuse the flu with a cold, which is much more common. Here are some differences between the two illnesses:

	COLD	FLU
Fever	rarely	always
Body ache	sometimes	often
Cough	produces **mucus**	usually dry

In general, the flu is a much stronger **viral** illness that usually forces its victims to stay in bed for several days. Influenza is also different from the bacterial and viral infections that some people call a "stomach flu". The vomiting and diarrhoea these infections cause are not common influenza symptoms.

The flu virus at work

The influenza virus targets cells in the host's **respiratory** system, which includes the nose and lungs. The effects of the disease, though, are felt throughout the entire body. From one to seven days after the virus enters, the infected person begins to feel the first symptoms of the flu. These usually include a high fever.

A fever starts when the body's white blood cells recognise the invading virus as foreign. In response, the white blood cells release a chemical that causes the body's temperature to rise. The surface of the body, however, gets colder when a fever begins. This leads to chills, which are another common flu symptom. Other chemicals in the **immune system** (the parts of the body that fight disease) create the body aches and headaches common with the flu. Coughs and a runny nose usually begin several days after the first symptoms strike.

Spreading the flu

In an infected person, the flu virus appears in the mist released when a person coughs or sneezes. The tiny particles of this respiratory fluid are called droplets. The virus spreads when a droplet enters the nose or mouth of another person. A person can also be infected if they touch a droplet that has landed on an object or person and then touch their own nose or mouth.

STOPPING THE SPREAD OF FLU

If you have the flu:
- Avoid going out in public.
- Cover your mouth when you sneeze or cough.
- Wash your hands after blowing your nose.

If you do *not* have the flu:
- Wash your hands often.
- Avoid people who are ill.
- Avoid touching your mouth, nose, or eyes.

Sneeze droplets can travel at speeds of 46 metres per second. Special high-speed cameras are needed to take a picture such as this.

WORD STORE   **epidemic** spread of a disease in one area
pandemic spread of a disease across large parts of the world

Scientists have discovered three types of influenza virus, now labelled A, B, and C. **Strains** of the type A virus are found in humans, pigs, birds, and other animals. Type A strains are the cause of most **epidemics** and all **pandemics** in humans. Type B affects only humans. It does not cause pandemics, but in a given year it might cause half of the world's known flu infections. Type C, also found in a variety of animals, creates only mild symptoms and does not cause epidemics.

Most flu vaccines are given with an injection into the muscle of the arm.

Who is at risk?

The influenza virus can strike anyone. Most people recover from the disease after a week or so. But for some people, the flu can last longer or lead to more severe health problems, such as **pneumonia**. Influenza can be deadly for young babies, the elderly, and pregnant women.

The swine flu of 2009 seemed to hit pregnant women especially hard, compared to the seasonal flu. In one case in England, a woman with severe swine flu symptoms had surgery so she could have her baby early. The baby survived, but the mother later died. Pregnant women were among the first people to receive vaccines for swine flu.

People with existing illnesses are also at high risk of serious problems if they catch the flu. Their bodies are too weak to fight off the disease or the pneumonia it can spark. With a strong pandemic virus, such as the 1918 flu, even healthy young adults might not be able to fight the disease.

A closer look

For several years after the 1918 flu pandemic, scientists thought bacteria caused influenza. But in 1930 US scientist Richard Shope learned that a virus caused influenza in pigs. Three years later, a team of British scientists led by Sir Christopher Andrewes used some of Shope's techniques to find the virus in humans. The history of fighting disease, and all of scientific research, follows this pattern. Scientists learn from earlier research and ideas in their field. They then use this to gain new knowledge.

Viruses could not be seen until the invention of powerful microscopes in the 1930s.

GENES AND LIFE

Scientists might not think viruses are living creatures, but the **ribonucleic acid (RNA)** they contain is important to life. In most organisms, RNA works with the chemical **deoxyribonucleic acid (DNA)** to direct the reproduction of cells. DNA contains genes, which tell an organism how to function. In humans and other organisms, genes also control the traits parents pass to their children. Such traits as a baby's eye colour and possible height are determined by the mixing of his or her parents' genes.

Once it finds a host, the influenza virus only needs RNA to reproduce. It acts the same way as genes do in humans. The RNA controls the virus's functions and passes on traits to new viruses created from the original virus.

WORD STORE   **DNA** chemicals containing trait-determining genes
Hemagglutinin (H) type of protein inside a flu virus

Knowing what caused the flu, the scientists began to study the virus in more detail. Today, researchers know that the virus is roughly the shape of a tiny ball. Like all viruses, an influenza virus has two major parts. A layer of **protein** surrounds a core material called ribonucleic acid (RNA). RNA is made up of chemicals that contain the instructions for an organism's function.

Emerging from the surface of the virus' protein cover are two kinds of spikes made of different proteins. These proteins are the tools the virus uses to attach to a host cell. **Hemagglutinin (H)** looks like a rod or cone, while the **neuraminidase (N)** protein has a round cap on top. Each of these proteins can appear in slightly different forms, and scientists have numbered each form. The combination of the different forms of the proteins leads to the names of different strains of influenza. The 1918 Spanish flu, for example, was H1N1. In recent years, the so-called bird, or avian, flu was labelled H5N1. The outbreak of swine flu in 2009 was caused by a new strain of H1N1.

The influenza virus

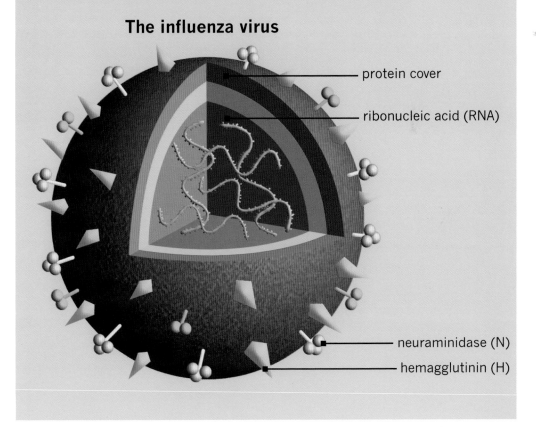

- protein cover
- ribonucleic acid (RNA)
- neuraminidase (N)
- hemagglutinin (H)

THE SEARCH FOR A
VACCINE

Even before scientists knew every detail about the structure of the flu virus itself, they began an important mission. They wanted to create a vaccine to prevent the flu. By the 1930s, vaccines had been used to prevent disease for more than 100 years. The first vaccine appeared long before scientists knew what viruses were or how vaccines fought them. Scientists did not discover viruses and how they caused illness until the end of the 1800s.

Usually given as an injection, a vaccine contains either weakened or dead forms of the virus itself. When people receive a vaccine today, they do not become ill from the dead or weakened virus. They can, however, feel **side effects**, such as soreness from the shot, nausea, or a fever. The virus in the vaccine then stirs the body's **immune system** into action. This prepares the body to fight live viruses later on.

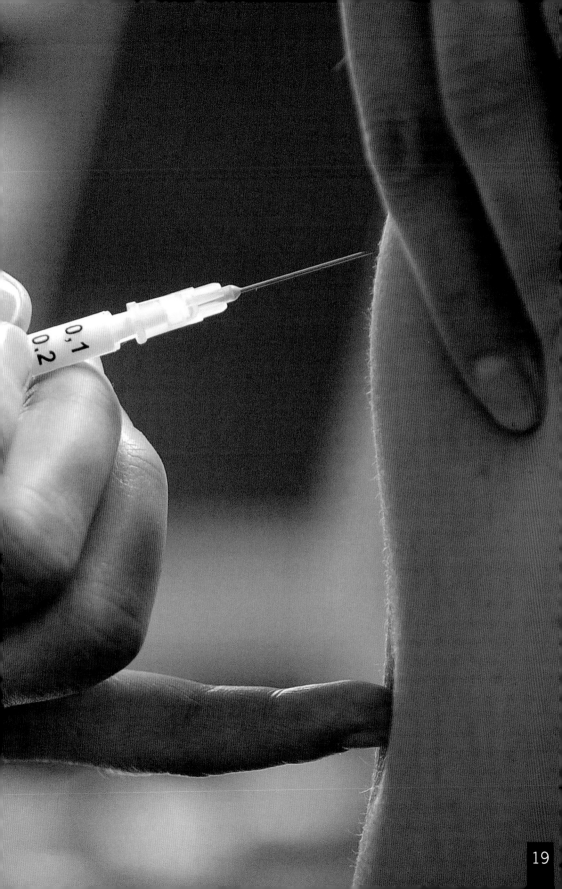

During his long scientific career, Thomas Francis also helped develop a vaccine to fight polio.

Francis goes to work

Soon after the flu virus was discovered, Thomas Francis and a team of US scientists began looking for a vaccine. Francis knew vaccines work with the immune system to prevent disease. When a vaccine enters the body, cells in the immune system release **proteins** called **antibodies**.

The body reacts this way whenever a foreign substance enters it. The antibodies are designed to seek out and destroy the invading substance. They remain in the body, ready to strike if the substance enters again in the future. The antibodies give immunity (protection) to the virus used to make the vaccine.

Creating the flu vaccine

Francis and his team grew the flu virus in chicken embryos, which are groups of cells that develop into a chicken. They did this because the virus can invade living cells. Inside the embryo, the virus grows rapidly, so scientists can produce enough of the virus to work with. The egg's shell and the embryo itself also help keep other micro-organisms away from the vaccine. Francis wanted to be sure that only the influenza virus was growing inside. Chicken embryos are still used to produce most influenza vaccines.

WORD STORE   **antibody** chemical that attacks invading micro-organisms

A key tool for all scientists is a hypothesis, or assumption. Scientists try to explain what happens in a body or what might happen in the future. Once they have a hypothesis, the scientists conduct tests to see if their ideas are right or not. Observing something, creating a theory to explain it, and then testing the theory is called the scientific method.

In the 1700s, English scientist Edward Jenner's hypothesis about smallpox led to the world's first vaccine. Jenner did not know about viruses. But he noticed that people infected with a disease called cowpox did not become ill during smallpox **epidemics**. Jenner's hypothesis was that cowpox somehow protected people from smallpox. To test his theory, he infected several people with cowpox. This made them slightly ill, but they quickly recovered. Then he infected them with the much deadlier smallpox. His test subjects did not develop smallpox.

Jenner called his treatment a vaccine, from the Latin word for the cowpox disease. Scientists now know that smallpox and cowpox are both created by similar viruses. Jenner's vaccination gave people immunity to smallpox, although his testing was extremely risky!

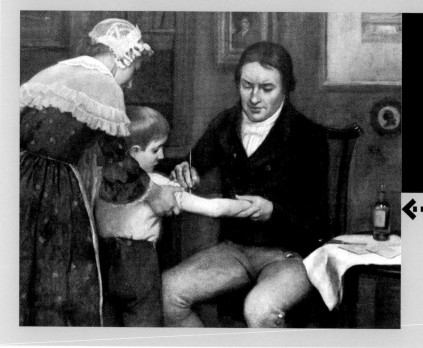

In 1796, Edward Jenner tested his smallpox vaccine on 8-year-old James Phipps, the son of a neighbour.

First tests

Francis did some of his first tests with ferrets. He inserted the influenza virus in the animals' noses. After the ferrets recovered, Francis tried to infect them again with the same **strain**. The ferrets, however, had developed antibodies that prevented them from getting the flu a second time.

WHY FERRETS?

When it comes to influenza, humans and ferrets have a lot in common. Ferrets can catch both the A and B types of the virus that infect humans. Once they are infected, ferrets experience similar **symptoms** to humans, and are ill for about the same length of time. Scientists study them to see how the disease is passed on and how new flu strains might affect people. Ferrets are also used to test new vaccines.

Testing with humans

Francis' next step was to kill the virus from the embryos and create a vaccine for human tests. A trial vaccine was tested in 1936 on 15 people. After receiving the flu vaccine, almost all of them developed immunity to the flu virus.

Francis wanted to test the vaccine on more people to make sure he had similar positive results. He told reporters, "It is very promising, but the campaign is far from over. It seems likely that vaccination may reduce the [effects] of influenza."

WORD STORE   placebo substance in a medical test that is non-medicinal

To test medicines and vaccines, scientists commonly use at least two different groups of people. One group usually receives a **placebo**, which is an injection or pill that does not contain the medicine being tested. The scientists want the people to think they are receiving the real medicine.

In one of Francis' flu vaccine tests, one group of people was exposed to a virus and not given the real vaccine. They were three times more likely to develop the flu than the test group that received the vaccine. But even in the second group, which received the real vaccine, many people exposed to the virus became ill.

The effort to create a more powerful vaccine went on as the United States entered World War II (1939–45). The US government hoped to prevent another **pandemic** like the one that struck in 1918. In 1942 Francis' team finally produced large amounts of a vaccine able to prevent both type A and B influenza viruses. Starting in 1944, the government gave the vaccine to soldiers, and the public began receiving it after the war.

The chart below shows the results of early vaccination testing, using both type A and B influenza viruses.

Influenza A				
	No. of people	Vaccinated	% with a temperature above 37.8°C (100°F)	% with a temperature above 38.3°C (101°F)
Group 1	36	No	50	25
Group 2	28	Yes	32	11
Group 3	21	Yes	14	no data

Influenza B				
	No. of people	Vaccinated	% with a temperature above 37.8°C (100°F)	% with a temperature above 38.3°C (101°F)
Group 1	27	No	41	22
Group 2	27	Yes	7	no data
Group 3	23	Yes	13	no data

A CHANGING VIRUS

Thanks to Edward Jenner's work with the smallpox vaccine (see page 21), the disease has disappeared from Earth. Only a few small samples remain in laboratories. Polio, another **viral** illness, is also almost gone because of an effective vaccine. But the influenza virus presents scientists with a more difficult medical problem.

Since the early days of influenza research, Thomas Francis and others noticed that different forms of the virus appear at any one time. The virus **mutates**, or changes itself, much more rapidly than other viruses do. This means that a new vaccine must be developed each year.

Because of this rapid change, scientists can only guess which **strains** of the virus they should put into a new vaccine. Michael Decker works for a major drug company as a **virologist**, a scientist who studies viruses. He said, "By the time you know what the right strain is, you can't do anything about it."

Even if scientists know people are getting ill from the type A virus, they cannot be sure which of the known **sub-types**, or smaller categories, it is. Sometimes a virus mutates so much it is totally different from any existing sub-type.

This photo shows an example of type A influenza virus, as seen through a powerful microscope.

Changing genes

The fact that genes mutate makes the search for flu vaccines a difficult task. Genes in any organism can mutate – for different reasons. An outside force, such as certain forms of energy or some chemicals, may damage the **DNA** inside the gene or the **RNA** inside the virus. This damage may cause a mutation, or change. The harmful change in the gene can also occur for no apparent reason.

In either case, the damaged **genetic** material is then passed on when the cell reproduces. In many organisms, a mutation creates health problems. In humans, for example, mutations of certain cells can lead to higher risks of heart disease.

Helpful mutations

Some mutations help organisms survive. Mutations play this role for the influenza virus. The flu virus produces a specific kind of **antibody** in a human host. The virus usually spreads around the world, seeking new hosts. If the same virus came back to a certain country after a year passed, it would be harder for it to find hosts. The people infected the first time would have antibodies that kill the virus.

Because of mutation, the flu virus is slightly different one year to the next. The mutation changes its **proteins**, which means the virus can infect the same person from year to year. With most other viral illnesses, a person who survives the illness develops a natural lifelong immunity to the disease. A single vaccine can also provide that immunity. But the constant changes in the flu virus means no one can ever be completely immune.

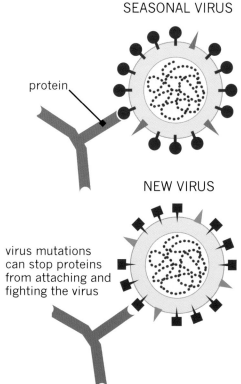

SEASONAL VIRUS

protein

NEW VIRUS

virus mutations can stop proteins from attaching and fighting the virus

A vaccine works by causing the body to produce proteins. These proteins attach to the virus and stop it from further infecting cells. However, the proteins may not be able to attach to a mutated virus.

WORD STORE   **genetic** related to genes

The common seasonal flu seems to spring from one part of the world. In 2008 British scientist Colin Russell released results that showed that East and Southeast Asia are the sources for most of the seasonal viruses. Russell explained, "Viruses circulate continuously in East and Southeast Asia by passing from country to country and then they are continuously showered out into the rest of the world."

Knowing this, scientists focus on the strains of virus that appear in Asia. Their research helps them create better vaccines for the flu that will strike North America and Europe in the following months.

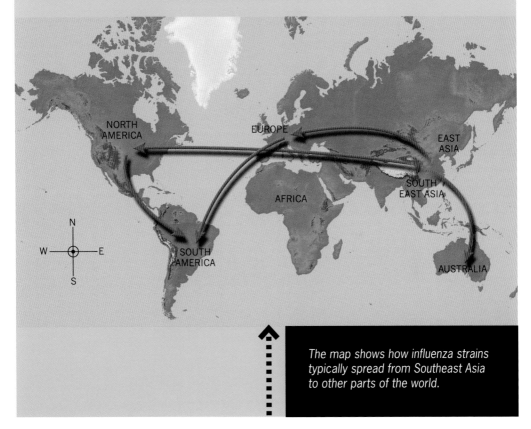

The map shows how influenza strains typically spread from Southeast Asia to other parts of the world.

Yearly protection

At times, the mutations in the flu virus from one year to another are slight. An infected person can develop partial immunity to a similar virus that appears the next year. But to be fully protected, people need a seasonal vaccine. Scientists predict which strains of the flu virus are likely to occur in the coming year. This is based mostly on the strains that infected people the year before.

A threat from animal viruses

The search for flu vaccines requires scientists to study animals as well as humans. Type A influenza, the most powerful kind, can affect a variety of animals. Most sub-types, though, only affect one or two kinds of animals. The virus that makes a person ill will not infect all other animals. Birds are the one exception: all the known types of type A influenza can strike birds.

Bird flu fears

Many wild birds spend much of their lives carrying influenza viruses. For most of them, the virus is not deadly. But when certain type A viruses spread to chickens and other poultry, they can quickly kill thousands of birds.

Ducks, such as these in China, can carry many different kinds of flu, but most will not affect humans.

A HIGHLY POTENT STRAIN

Seasonal influenza usually kills when an infected person's **immune system** becomes too weak to fight off other illnesses. Bird flu, however, can occasionally kill healthy people. The virus can infect the brain, and, at times lead to confusion or death. The virus can also cause the immune system to react so strongly that it directly damages the lungs. Bird flu is so strong that it has been known to kill cats, which usually do not get ill from other type A influenza strains.

Some of these types of bird flu can also move on to infect other animals, such as humans. Knowing this, scientists have focused on the possible effects of types of bird flu on people.

Cases of avian, or bird, flu in humans began reappearing in 1997. The strain that affected humans is called H5N1. Over the next decade, only several hundred people caught the disease. However, the percentage who died was high, compared to other strains of influenza.

Luckily, bird flu did not spread easily among people. Scientists learned that the virus only attacked cells deep in the lungs. Droplets in an infected person's sneeze or cough were not likely to contain the virus. However, scientists feared mutations in the virus could make it more likely to spread among humans.

Bird flu vaccines arrive

Scientists began testing a vaccine for bird flu in 2005. The researchers soon learned that they needed large amounts of the virus to create an effective vaccine. Producing that much of the virus took longer than it takes to make seasonal flu vaccines. Researchers kept looking for better ways to prevent the spread of H5N1.

Malik Peiris, a scientist in Hong Kong, worked on a project that combined proteins from the H5N1 virus with a smallpox vaccine. He said in 2009 that the new vaccine produced a lot of H5N1 antibodies and "the speed of antibody response was far higher with this strategy" than with the earlier H5N1 vaccine. Peiris found these results after testing the new method on mice. He then looked for similar results in ferrets and monkeys before finally testing it on humans.

A larger threat

The jump of a flu virus from birds to humans is not the only danger people face. Both avian flu and type A flu that infect humans can strike pigs. On rare occasions, the RNA of two or more different viruses blend together inside the pig's cells. This blending creates a virus slightly different from others that have infected humans before. Scientists call the blending an antigenic shift. An **antigen** is any substance that leads to the production of antibodies.

The pig now contains this new, blended virus. The greatest medical problem comes if the new strain moves from pigs to humans. As with avian flu, people do not have antibodies that can fight the disease. But unlike bird flu, the blended viruses from pigs can often spread easily from one person to another in respiratory droplets. The risk of a **pandemic** is high. Scientists have to act quickly to identity the new strain and begin to make a vaccine.

Daniel Perez is a virologist at the University of Maryland in the United States. He led research that helped ease some of the fears about a mutating swine flu. Perez infected ferrets with both H1N1 and two kinds of seasonal flu. The swine flu virus did not combine with the other strains to create a new virus.

But the H1N1 was stronger than the other strains – it reproduced faster and was more easily spread. This suggested swine flu could still be a health risk. Perez said his lab work "underscores the need for vaccinating against the pandemic flu virus . . . the far greater communicability [ability to spread] of the pandemic virus serves as a clearly blinking warning light".

This blending of several viral strains led to the 1918 flu pandemic. It also sparked the swine flu, or H1N1, pandemic of 2009. Scientists feared that the new H1N1 virus would continue to change once it entered humans. It could blend with existing seasonal viruses and create a "super flu".

By autumn 2009, companies had already made several hundred million doses of vaccine for swine flu. Tests showed they were effective in preventing swine flu. But further mutations in the virus would have made those vaccines less effective in preventing the flu. Scientists kept studying samples of the virus to look for any important mutations.

FIGHTING THE FLU
TODAY

Studying new types of flu and the seasonal flu that strikes each year is the job of thousands of scientists around the world. Governments, private hospitals, and universities hire these researchers, who share information about their work. Here are just a few of the recent projects that are working towards a better flu vaccine.

In Hong Kong, scientists seek volunteers who have survived swine flu. The doctors take **antibodies** from the patients' blood to create a special vaccine. This vaccine is given to others suffering from severe cases of swine flu. The same process has been shown to work in treating mice infected with avian flu.

Researchers in Leicester test the strength of the swine flu vaccine. They have learned that just one shot should be enough to protect most people.

In Australia, the Czech Republic, and many other nations, drug companies use several billion chicken eggs to grow the seasonal and **pandemic** vaccines used to fight influenza.

A research team in Boston, USA, studies the **proteins** of the influenza virus. The new knowledge the team gains might lead to a new kind of vaccine. This universal vaccine could mean the end of yearly flu shots for hundreds of millions of people.

Scientists performing research at the World Influenza Centre in London. Cabinets like the ones in this photo are used when scientists are working with very dangerous micro-organisms, such as the flu virus.

Watching the world's health

In this international effort to battle influenza, individual governments provide funding for research. But the World Health Organization (WHO) helps oversee much of the information gathered. The organization is part of the United Nations. The WHO works with scientists around the world to prepare the yearly seasonal vaccine. The WHO's experts also watch for outbreaks of pandemic **strains**.

More than 90 nations have influenza centres that collect samples of the influenza virus from sick people. The samples are sent to five main WHO centres. Researchers at the centres look for rare strains that could cause a pandemic. Each virus has unique **genetic** material, so researchers can tell one strain from another. The WHO tracks where strains such as the avian and swine flu occur. Their scientists use this information to determine if a pandemic is likely to happen or has already occurred.

The search for the seasonal vaccine

In hospitals around the world, doctors take small samples of **mucus** from people infected with the flu. Doctors use these tests to confirm a patient has the flu. Some of the flu tests doctors use can give a result in 15 minutes. Although not always accurate, these rapid tests are helpful for telling doctors if a patient has the flu, rather than a simple cold or an infection caused by bacteria.

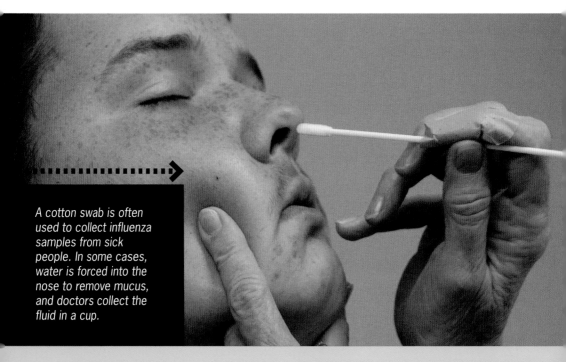

A cotton swab is often used to collect influenza samples from sick people. In some cases, water is forced into the nose to remove mucus, and doctors collect the fluid in a cup.

THE WORLD HEALTH ORGANIZATION'S SIX PHASES OF HUMAN INFLUENZA OUTBREAKS

Phase 1: No known animal flu viruses are found in humans.

Phase 2: An animal virus is found in humans.

Phase 3: Cases of animal-to-human infection grow, but there is no spread of the virus from one person to another.

Phase 4: The virus spreads among people in one area.

Phase 5: The virus spreads among people in at least two countries within a particular region.

Phase 6: The virus spreads to another region beyond the area where it was found in Phase 5, and a pandemic is declared.

Growing a virus in the laboratory is the best way for scientists to learn which strain is at work. Growing the virus, using cells in a lab, produces something called a **viral** culture. The culture takes up to 10 days to produce a result. But the scientists then have enough of the virus to see if it matches a common strain or might be a stronger influenza virus.

At the WHO and national influenza centres, scientists collect information from the patient tests. They learn which of thousands of different flu strains were the most common during the recent flu season. That information helps them decide which vaccines should be developed for the following year.

Two flu seasons

The world has two major flu seasons, centred around the winter months. In the Northern Hemisphere, which includes North America and Europe, winter starts in December and ends in March. That time is the peak flu season. In the Southern Hemisphere, winter starts in June and ends in September. WHO experts might recommend two different seasonal vaccines, depending on which ones struck in each hemisphere.

For the Northern Hemisphere, the scientists meet in February to decide which flu strains should go into the vaccine for the coming season. Each vaccine contains two kinds of the more harmful type A virus and one of type B.

In the lab

WHO scientists prepare strains of the flu virus that will go into the seasonal vaccine. The viruses are first grown in labs. These strains are called reference strains. Each strain is produced separately. The three are later combined to make the vaccine. The reference strains are grown in chicken embryos or cells taken from the kidneys of chickens.

In the "factory"

The WHO gives small samples of the reference strains to private medical companies that make the vaccine. These samples are called seeds, because they are used to grow the virus used to make the vaccines. Most of the companies use chicken eggs to grow the vaccines.

The vaccine plants must be kept very clean, to make sure no harmful micro-organisms enter the vaccine. Workers wear hats, gloves, and special clothes designed to keep out germs. Even the eggs are cleaned with a special cleaning spray.

The eggs are then placed in a warming tray, so the virus can grow. After several days, the virus is "harvested" from the egg and killed. Special machines help remove egg cells from the vaccine. This process, called **purification**, is repeated several times.

Preparing the seasonal vaccine

Month	Select strains	Produce virus	Purify and test	Fill and pack doses	Ship vaccine	Vaccinate patients
January	Select strains					
February	Select strains					
March						
April		Produce virus				
May						
June						
July						
August			Purify and test			
September				Fill and pack doses	Ship vaccine	
October						
November						
December						Vaccinate patients
January						

WORD STORE **purification** removing unwanted cells from a vaccine
side effect unwanted reaction to a drug

In Edward Jenner's day, he was able to simply round up a few local people to test his smallpox vaccine. No government officials watched over his trial. Today, though, countries have laws that set rules for testing vaccines on humans. Research hospitals and universities then set up their own groups that make sure these rules are followed. The rules include:

- All people who take part in medical tests must volunteer.
- They must be told of any possible harmful side effects of the vaccine being tested.
- The information gathered must be more important than any possible risk to the volunteers.

The manufacturer and government officials then test the vaccine to make sure the virus is dead and contains enough viral proteins to be effective.

In further tests, small groups of people are given the vaccine to make sure there are no **side effects**. Dr Gary Nabel, of the National Institute of Allergy and Infectious Diseases, says, "When you have a vaccine that you're giving to a healthy person, there's great value that we place on safety. Where side effects are often tolerated for medicines, with vaccines we have a very low tolerance for them."

Preparing for use

Once the tests are done, the medical companies prepare millions of doses of the vaccines. The vaccine goes into tiny glass containers called vials or directly into the needles used to give injections. In the Northern Hemisphere, these doses begin to be shipped out to hospitals, clinics, and private doctors during August and September. Doctors begin giving the vaccine to patients in October. The vaccine needs about two weeks to create enough antibodies to protect the patients from catching the flu.

In September 2009, a lab worker prepared swine flu vaccines.

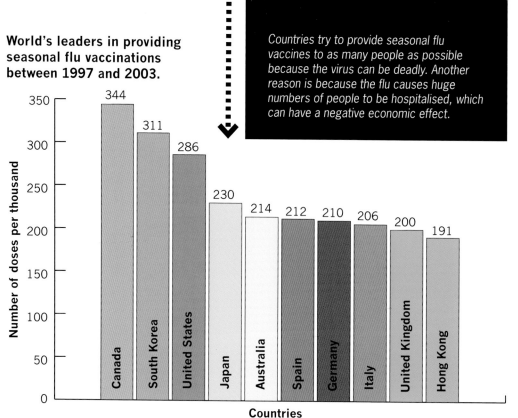

World's leaders in providing seasonal flu vaccinations between 1997 and 2003.

Countries try to provide seasonal flu vaccines to as many people as possible because the virus can be deadly. Another reason is because the flu causes huge numbers of people to be hospitalised, which can have a negative economic effect.

Number of doses per thousand

Canada 344
South Korea 311
United States 286
Japan 230
Australia 214
Spain 212
Germany 210
Italy 206
United Kingdom 200
Hong Kong 191

Countries

A new approach

Back in the days of Thomas Francis, all flu vaccines used dead viruses. Starting in the 1950s, Dr John Maassab, of the University of Michigan in the United States, sought to make a vaccine that used a live, weakened flu virus. Decades later, he said, "I was inspired by the success . . . of another live-virus vaccine in preventing polio." Maassab knew that some people who received the killed-virus flu vaccination still became ill. He hoped the weakened virus might be more effective.

Long process

Maassab and his assistants spent decades trying to create a weakened flu virus that would work in a vaccine. They finally found that temperature played a key role. The influenza virus reproduces best in the lungs. The temperature is warmer there than in a person's nose.

In the lab, Maassab was able to grow weakened virus strains at lower temperatures. He then created a mist that shot the virus into the nose. The virus survived there but was too weak to cause the flu. The vaccine also created antibodies that remained in the nose. Those antibodies could then kill an active virus of the same strain when it entered a person's nose. It did this before it could reach the lungs and cause the flu.

Test and approval

Starting in the 1970s, Maassab and other US scientists tested the new vaccine on children. Only one per cent of the children who received the vaccine, called FluMist, became ill. Many more who received a **placebo** caught the flu. Maassab also learned that the weakened-virus vaccine gives longer and better immunity than a killed-virus vaccine.

During the tests, some children reported a runny nose or sore throat. But these were considered mild side effects, given the value of the vaccine. FluMist was approved for use in 2003, and millions of doses are now given out each year, mainly to children and young adults.

> **"**I hope that the success of the approaches I have developed will continue the development of live vaccines for other **respiratory** viruses that cause disease and disability.**"**
>
> *John Maassab*

EAT YOUR VACCINE?

As painless as nasal vaccines are, Barry Marshall wants one that is even easier to use. The Australian scientist is working on a flu vaccine people would swallow. He hopes to take genetic material from a virus and attach it to bacteria that easily live in the stomach. A person would swallow a pill with the bacteria and the virus. The vaccine would then create antibodies, just as existing vaccines do. The new vaccine has worked on mice, and Marshall began testing it on humans in 2009.

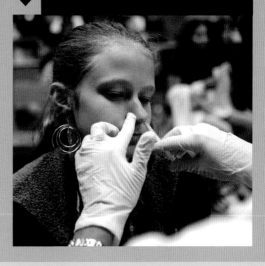

Nasal vaccines like FluMist are commonly used to vaccinate children, but scientists hope to find even easier ways to give vaccines.

FIGHTING
SWINE FLU

The virus was too slow.

That is what scientists noticed in July 2009, as they tried to prepare a vaccine for swine flu. Although the virus spread quickly around the globe, it was a slow grower in the laboratory. Inside chicken embryos, the virus was only growing up to half as quickly as the seasonal viruses used for vaccines.

During 2009 scientists took all the same steps they normally do to prepare the seasonal flu vaccine. But this time, speed was important. Normally, they had up to 10 months to identify the **strain**, go through the **purification** process, and test vaccines. This time, the doctors wanted a vaccine before the regular autumn flu season began. The drugmakers would have to produce both the seasonal and swine flu vaccines at the same time.

In November production still had not reached the numbers some officials wanted. In the United States, Thomas Frieden of the Centers for Disease Control said, "We're having a steady increase in the availability of vaccines, but not nearly as rapidly as we would have liked."

The swine flu virus, shown here developing inside a chicken embryo.

Safety issues

Even with the need for speed, the scientists had to follow strict safety rules. In clinics or hospitals where they collected samples taken from sick people, workers wore face masks and protective glasses. In labs where they worked with the virus strains, scientists did most of their work inside special glass cabinets. The researchers put their hands under a piece of glass that prevented any substance from splashing on them. Special air filters kept the virus from escaping from the cabinet.

First doses – and concerns

Finally, in October, several million doses of FluMist for swine flu were available. Killed-virus vaccines soon followed. The World Health Organization told health workers to receive the vaccine first. They needed to be well to help take care of people who caught the flu. In the United States, officials also urged children to get vaccinated first. If children become ill, they often spread the flu to their parents, who then spread it to other adults. Pregnant women, the elderly, and people who were already ill were also told to get the vaccination as soon as possible.

In the United Kingdom, the government planned to vaccinate the entire population against swine flu. But even though the injection would be free, some people resisted getting it. Some nurses, in particular, seemed to fear the vaccine's safety. Nurses were a priority for vaccination, because they were at risk of being exposed to the flu in hospitals. But some of them believed the new vaccine had not been properly tested.

At the same time, the **media** reported on the rising death toll, though the number was not as high as had been feared. Most of the deaths seemed to come from the at-risk groups – pregnant woman or people with existing illnesses. The government used the media to spread an important message: the vaccine was safe and people should get it.

WORD STORE **antiviral** substance that attacks a virus once it invades
mutate when an organism changes genetically

ANTIVIRAL DRUGS

After you catch the flu, you cannot take a medicine to kill it. But **antiviral** drugs can ease the **symptoms**. In some cases, they can also prevent the flu in a person who has been near someone infected with the virus.

Four antiviral drugs have been developed to treat seasonal flu. In May 2009 researchers learned that two of them could ease the symptoms of swine flu. But in the following months, the virus **mutated** and was better able to resist the drugs. However, scientists saw that this mutation had one good result for people. The mutated virus was less likely to pass from one person to another.

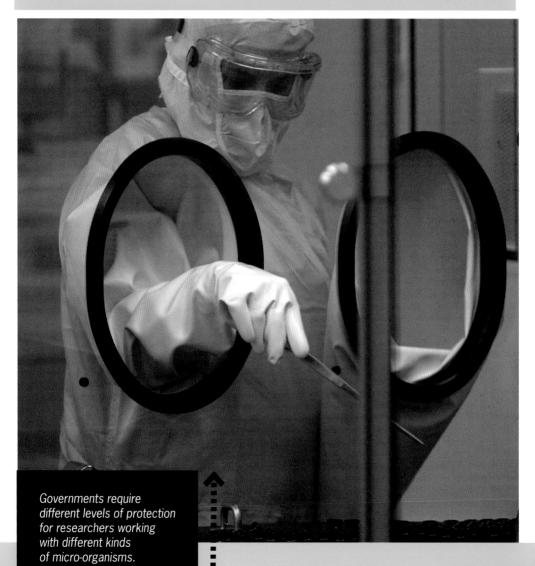

Governments require different levels of protection for researchers working with different kinds of micro-organisms.

Learning from the past

Fears caused by the swine flu turned attention back to the 1918 flu **pandemic**. Scientists had already done important work on the virus, helping them understand killer flus. A long-dead Alaskan woman provided some of the key clues.

The woman had died from the 1918 Spanish flu, a different version of the 2009 H1N1 virus, or swine flu. Her body had been buried in partially frozen ground. The cold earth and the woman's own body fat helped preserve some of the virus. Her body was uncovered in 1997, and scientists began studying the virus that remained in her lungs. Two smaller samples had already been taken from soldiers who died during the pandemic.

Useful discoveries

In a laboratory Dr Jeffery Taubenberger, of the US Armed Forces Institute of Pathology, and a team of scientists studied the 1918 virus. They were able to recreate the sequence, or code, of **RNA** inside it. With that code, they created a new version of the same virus so they could study it. Another team of scientists led by Dr Gary Nabel, of the US National Institute of Allergy and Infectious Diseases, then tried to make a vaccine that could stop the spread of the 1918 virus.

A successful test

In 2006 Nabel made this announcement about the Spanish flu: "The good news is that it's a bad virus but it's not resistant to vaccination." His team had found a vaccine for it that worked in mice.

Instead of using a whole killed or weakened virus, they created the vaccine using **genetic** material from the virus. The scientists then exposed both vaccinated and unvaccinated mice to the 1918 virus. All the vaccinated mice lived, while the ones that did not get the vaccine died.

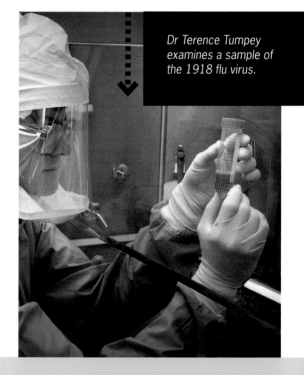

Dr Terence Tumpey examines a sample of the 1918 flu virus.

Vaccines based on a virus' genetic material are called DNA vaccines. After his work with mice and the 1918 H1N1 virus, Dr Nabel began testing a DNA vaccine for bird flu on humans. Later tests with animals showed a DNA vaccine might prevent different forms of bird flu. In 2009 a company tested a DNA vaccine for swine flu. The DNA vaccines can be developed faster than ones that grow in chicken eggs.

Further study

In 2007 Dr Terrence Tumpey of the US Center for Disease Control announced results of his work on the 1918 virus. He found that making small changes in the virus' H protein made it harder for the virus to spread. Tumpey explained why he and other scientists are so interested in the 1918 virus: "It's important to actually study a pandemic virus to help us better understand other influenza viruses with pandemic potential."

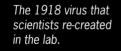

The 1918 virus that scientists re-created in the lab.

THE FUTURE OF
FLU
VACCINES

Imagine it is the year 2020. You wait for your doctor to give you a flu vaccine. When it is over, you smile, knowing you will never have to get another seasonal vaccination.

Sound like a dream? Not to the scientists working on a so-called universal flu vaccine. Their goal is to create a vaccine that would fight the ever-changing **strains** of seasonal flu. At first, you might still have to get a seasonal vaccine, plus the universal. The second vaccine would help fight off strains that are not contained in the seasonal vaccination.

The goal of a lifetime vaccination from one injection might not be reachable. The first universal vaccines tested did not completely prevent the flu, as seasonal vaccines can. But the universal vaccines did limit the effects and the spread of the seasonal flu. Future universal vaccines should be more effective. They should at least reduce the number of times a person needs an injection. Extra, or booster, vaccinations might be needed every 10 years. Ideally, the universal flu vaccine would also work against **pandemic** strains of influenza.

A researcher holds up a new, needle-free flu vaccine. Scientists are working to fully develop vaccines like this that can be applied simply by sticking a patch on a patient's skin!

A key to the universal vaccine

A special "library" in a laboratory in Massachusetts, USA holds 27 billion **antibodies**. Years ago, Wayne Marasco of Harvard Medical School and his assistants took the cells from human volunteers. Since then, Marasco and other scientists have used the antibodies to try to kill new strains of influenza.

Marasco found 10 antibodies in the library that killed the H5N1 bird flu in mice. To his surprise, the antibodies also worked with other strains. Marasco, like other scientists, assumed the flu virus changed too quickly for one antibody to fight different strains.

Marasco and other scientists then looked more closely at an antibody as it attached to one of the virus's **proteins**. The antibody did not cling to the top of the protein, which **mutates** quickly. Instead the antibody was attached to the stem of the protein. This part contains information that the virus needs to live. Rubin Donis of the Centers for Disease Control worked with Marasco. He said, "The virus cannot mutate [the stem] because by doing so, it would commit suicide."

Scientists quickly saw the value of Marasco's work. New vaccines that targeted the stem of the protein instead of the changing top would work against many strains. Scientists would have the universal vaccine. However, learning about the protein stem was just the first step. Researchers still had to create a vaccine able to target the stem.

Another approach

In the United Kingdom, scientist Sarah Gilbert of Oxford University looked for another way to fight many different flu viruses. She says, "The sooner we have a universal vaccine the better because we can stop worrying about what the next pandemic will be."

Deaths resulting from flu strains

Annual worldwide deaths from seasonal flu	25,000–500,000
1918 Spanish flu	40 million or more
1957 Asian flu	2 million
1968 Hong Kong flu	1 million
2009 Swine flu	13,663

As a first step in fighting new flu strains, Wayne Marasco and others began working on a new **antiviral** drug. The drug has antibodies that target the stem, which does not mutate in the flu virus protein. Scientists use mice to produce enough of the antibodies for the drugs. The mice have their genes altered so they can create antibodies that are safe for humans. Marasco planned to test the new antiviral drug on ferrets before testing it on humans. The photo below shows a strain of seasonal flu.

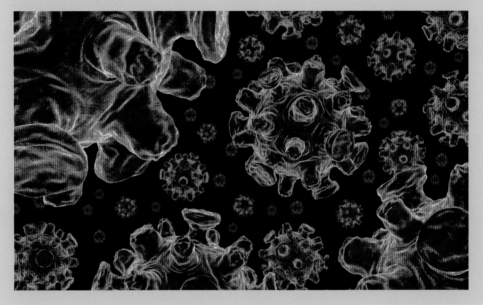

Gilbert focused on cells that are always part of the human **immune system**. These cells, known as T-cells, have a natural ability to fight the flu virus. They target a part of the virus that does not mutate fast enough to keep the swarming T-cells from killing it. However, the ability of T-cells to kill a flu virus weakens over time. The vaccine Gilbert is working on would boost T-cells when a virus enters the body. Her research shows some people can resist the flu just with these cells and not antibodies.

An ongoing search

The fast-changing flu virus presents a much harder challenge than smallpox or polio did. A universal vaccine might not completely prevent infection, but, according to Suzanne Epstein of the US Food and Drug Administration, "What it can do is greatly reduce disease and spread and **symptoms**." Scientists will continue their mission to help humans cope with what is often a deadly disease.

TIMELINE OF
FLU VACCINES

1796 English scientist Edward Jenner tests his vaccine for smallpox.

1857 French scientist Louis Pasteur suggests that micro-organisms cause some illnesses. This is known as the germ theory of disease.

1885 Pasteur tests a vaccine for rabies (a deadly viral disease).

1918 The Spanish flu epidemic begins, killing more than 40 million people.

1930 US scientist Richard Shope finds a flu virus in a pig.

1933 British scientists led by Sir Christopher Andrewes identify the flu virus in humans for the first time.

1942 US scientists led by Thomas Francis develop the first flu vaccine; Francis soon learns the virus mutates quickly, so the vaccine must be changed from year to year.

1952 US scientist Jonas Salk tests a polio vaccine that uses a dead virus.

1957 The Asian flu pandemic begins.

1958 US scientist Albert Sabin develops a polio vaccine that uses a weakened virus.

1963 A measles vaccine developed by US scientists Samuel Katz and John F Enders is approved for public use.

1968 The Hong Kong flu pandemic begins.

1971 Children begin receiving a single shot that combines vaccines for mumps, measles, and rubella.

1976 Severe illnesses in the United States are linked to a swine flu vaccine, ending the vaccination programme.

1988 Japan and South Korea approve the use of a vaccine for chicken pox.

1997 The H5N1 avian flu begins appearing in humans. The body of an Alaskan woman buried in frozen ground is removed. Scientists find remains of the 1918 flu virus in her lungs.

2003 FluMist, a nasal flu vaccine, is approved for human use.

2009 First reports of "swine flu" deaths are reported in Mexico. The World Health Organization announces that H1N1, also called swine flu, has reached a pandemic stage.

"We are in much better shape than we were in 1918. First of all, we know that influenza viruses exist and we can analyse them and watch their emergence and evolution. Secondly, health care has come a long way. We have the influenza vaccines, which are obviously the most important factor of our current weapons against influenza viruses. So all of those things could be put into motion. The problem would be to do it fast enough."

Scientist Jeffery Taubenberger, from the 1998 PBS documentary Influenza 1918.

GLOSSARY

antibody chemical that attacks micro-organisms that invade a life form

antigen substance that leads to the production of antibodies

antiviral substance that attacks a virus once it enters a body

deoxyribonucleic acid (DNA) chemicals that contain the genes that determine an organism's traits

epidemic spread of a disease in one area

genetic related to genes

hemagglutinin (H) type of protein inside a flu virus

immune system organs and cells in the body that help fight disease

media organizations that produce news reports through printed or electronic methods

mucus slippery fluid produced in various parts of the body, including the respiratory system

mutate when an organism becomes different because of changes to its genetic material

neuraminidase (N) type of protein found inside a flu virus

pandemic spread of a disease across large parts of the world

particle tiny piece of material

pathogen micro-organism that causes disease

placebo non-medicinal substance given instead of a real chemical during a medical test

pneumonia lung disease caused by a variety of pathogens, including bacteria and viruses

protein combination of chemicals in cells and other parts of the body that help them function

purification process of removing unwanted cells from a vaccine

respiratory related to parts of the body used in breathing

ribonucleic acid (RNA) chemicals that contain instructions for an organism's function

side effect unintended, possibly harmful reaction produced by a drug

strain slightly different version of a virus type

sub-type smaller category of something within a larger group

symptom outward sign of a disease in an infected person

viral related to a virus

virologist scientist who studies viruses

FIND OUT MORE

BOOKS

Analyse This! Understanding the Scientific Method, Susan Glass (Heinemann Library, 2007)

Epidemics and Plagues, Richard Walker (Kingfisher, 2006)

Great Minds of Science: Edward Jenner, Ana Maria Rodriguez (Enslow, 2006)

Great Scientists: Louis Pasteur, Liz Miles (Heinemann Library, 2008)

Killing Germs, Saving Lives: The Quest for the First Vaccines, Glen Phelan (National Geographic, 2006)

The Impact of Science and Technology: Health and Medicine, Anne Rooney (Franklin Watts, 2009)

WEBSITES

Famous People
www.bbc.co.uk/history/historic_figures/jenner_edward.shtml
Find out more about Edward Jenner on this web page. You can also find information about another famous scientist, Louis Pasteur, by using the alphabet link.

The Guardian
www.guardian.co.uk/uk/interactive/2008/jan/03/flu
This site shows how the flu pandemic took hold in Britain in 1918.

BBC History
www.bbc.co.uk/history/british/middle_ages/black_01.shtml
Follow the Black Death as it moved through Britain.

NHS: Immunisation History
www.immunisation.nhs.uk/About_Immunisation/History/Introduction
Read all about the history of immunisation.

Antibiotics and Immunisation
www.bbc.co.uk/schools/ks3bitesize/science/organisms_behaviour_
health/disease/revise6.shtml
Check your understanding of immunisation on this web page.

WHO Global Influenza Programme
www.who.int/csr/disease/influenza/en/index.html
Learn about how the WHO is dealing with influenza.

TOPICS TO LEARN MORE ABOUT

- **The people who oppose vaccines**
  Since Edward Jenner's time, some people have opposed the
  use of vaccines. Who are some of the people who oppose giving
  vaccines today, especially to children? What are their fears? What
  do scientists say against their arguments?

- **The Black Death**
  A disease called the Plague, or the Black Death, caused the worst
  pandemic of all time. Learn more about this deadly disease and the
  vaccine finally developed to fight it.

- **The 1918 flu pandemic**
  Did this terrible outbreak of flu affect your community? Do research
  to find out if there were many deaths. See if your family knows of
  any relatives who might have been affected.

INDEX